UNLOCKING HORNS
COURAGEOUS CONFLICT AT WORK

by: BILL TREASURER, FOUNDER, GIANT LEAP CONSULTING, INC.

LITTLE LEAPS
PRESS

OBJECTIVES

CONFLICT MANAGEMENT WORKSHOP

Discuss the importance of conflict resolution relative to your career

Practice improving how you deal with conflict, using your own interpersonal challenges and dilemmas.

Understand various sources of conflict

Learn practical ways to make conflict productive instead of destructive.

Understand various approaches for preventing conflict from occurring in the first place.

DEAR READER,

Conflict is! There's no escaping that reality at work. Whether you're a new leader having to confront poor performance issues, or a seasoned leader having to protect your organization's interests as you negotiate with an over-dominant customer, to be successful, you're going to have to be skilled at engaging in conflict. Running away is not an option! Well, it is, but it's a cowardly one!

Fundamentally, there are really only two kinds of conflict: productive or destructive. The reason people many people shy away from conflict is because they've witnessed or experienced the painful effects of destructive conflict. Poorly managed conflict is costly. At best, destructive conflict results in hurt feelings. At worst, mismanaged and destructive conflict ends in workplace violence. So getting conflict right, and keeping it productive, is supremely important.

The good news is, productive conflict is the sign of a healthy business! Productive conflict yields high-integrity and well-considered decisions that have been shaped and tested by multiple perspectives and viewpoints. Productive conflict yields transparency, where people don't swallow or hide their true opinions and perspectives. Productive conflict creates shared accountability where people don't fear confronting teammates who aren't carrying their weight, or are not upholding the organization's values. Productive conflict is good business. It just takes courage on your part!

My promise to you is that this workbook won't waste your time! Whether you've purchased Unlocking Horns to get ready-to-deploy ideas for keeping your own conflicts productive, or if you're using this resource as part of Giant Leap Consulting's conflict optimization workshop, the tips and approaches you're about to be introduced to have been road-tested by people as discerning, smart, and impatient as you! You want stuff that works now, and you've come to the right place.

Keep this in mind as you progress through Unlocking Horns: the strongest and most valued and business relationships are fortified and developed through conflict. Learning to how to engage with people fairly, squarely, and maturely-especially when you're viewpoints are at odds-is how you come to respect and trust one another. Strong relationships can withstand a good fight. Heck, they require them!

Here's to having lots and lots of business opportunities worth fighting for!

Bill Treasurer

BILL TREASURER
Founder, Giant Leap Consulting, Inc.
(GiantLeapConsulting.com)

> **"Conflict is the gadfly of thought. It stirs us to observation and memory. It instigates to invention. It shocks us out of sheeplike passivity…"**

— *John Dewey*
(American Philosopher, Psychologist and Educator, 1859-1952)

JUST THE FACTS

1 92% of leaders say that teamwork is critical to their success. 23% say their team is effective.

2 $359 billion in paid hours or the equivalent of 385 million working days are lost each year to workplace conflict.

3 Estimates suggest that 2.8 hours each week are spent dealing with workplace conflict.

4 In the mid 1970's, it was estimated that 30% of a managers time was spent dealing with conflict. 30 years later, a study showed that 42% of a manager's time is spent on reaching agreement with others when conflicts occur... the trend is getting worse!

5 Almost 60% of employees in the U.S. have never received basic conflict management and dispute resolution training.

6 Every year, 2 million American workers report having been victims of workplace violence. In 2014, 409 people were fatally injured in work-related attacks, according to the U.S. Bureau of Labor Statistics.

7 85% of employees deal with conflict on some level. 29 % of employees deal with it almost constantly.

8 76% of employees who receive conflict management training experience positive outcomes from conflict.

9 In a study conducted with 6000 complainants at MIT, 75% say that during a workplace conflict, they lack the skills they need to change the situation effectively.

CONFLICTS IMPACT

Think about the conflicts you've seen or experienced in your job.
What are some healthy things that have resulted from these conflicts?

HEALTHY RESULTS OF CONFLICT

Now think of the unhealthy impacts that conflict has had.

HEALTHY RESULTS OF CONFLICT

"In the frank expression of conflicting opinions lies the greatest promise of wisdom…"
—Louis Brandeis

CONFLICT HANDLING MODES:
DOS & DON'TS

- ✓ Create a "partnership" atmosphere
- ✓ Establish conflict guidelines and guiding principles
- ✓ Acknowledge the other person's point of view
- ✓ Focus on points of agreement
- ✓ Keep and open mind
- ✓ Ask for clarification
- ✓ Discuss Pros and Cons
- ✓ Paraphrase or use role reversal
- ✓ Separate people from ideas
- ✓ Articulate "interests"

- ✗ Bring up past injustices
- ✗ Interrupt before a point is made
- ✗ Attack ideas
- ✗ Be intimidating
- ✗ Be defensive of your own ideas
- ✗ Take sides
- ✗ Argue "positions"
- ✗ …forget to shake on it

LANGUAGE FOR PRODUCTIVE CONFLICT

Impatience "Can you move on? You've said the same thing four times now."	**Patience** "I can tell you're concerned about this, because you've referred to it multiple times. What would it take for you to resolve this issue?"
Critical of the Person "You just don't listen, do you? I've told you more than once that you can't make that decision without consulting me, yet here we are again."	**Critical of the Performance** "You and I have reviewed the approval process before. It is not acceptable that you continue to sign off without involving me."
Unsupporting "Well, of course you feel like a failure. When you don't think things through you crash and burn."	**Supporting** I know you feel badly, but there are probably many valuable learnings in this experience. How might you do it differently next time?"
Unaccepting "I'm sorry, but you're dead wrong."	**Accepting** "I see the situation a bit differently, but here are the points that you made that I do agree with…"
Advice-Giving "You need to see a therapist about this."	**Withholding Advice** "What are some ways that you can confront this issue head on?"
Judgmental "That's a foolish thing to say about yourself."	**Non-Judgmental** "That's a discouraging thing to hear you say. I wonder if you could reframe the situation to see it differently?"

CONDITIONS THAT PROMOTE CONFLICT RESOLUTION

BOTH PARTIES IN CONFLICT MUST SET THE
STAGE FOR CONFLICT RESOLUTION. TOGETHER, THEY MUST:

SHARE INTEREST IN RESOLVING THE CONFLICT

MUTUALLY DEFINE AND UNDERSTAND THE PROBLEM

CONTINUALLY FOCUS ON THE PROBLEM VS. PERSONALITIES

ALLOW FOR A SPECIFIC AMOUNT OF TIME FOR CONSTRUCTIVE "VENTING"

RECOGNIZE THAT BOTH PARTIES ARE PART OF THE PROBLEM & SOLUTION

BE WILLING TO PURSUE WIN-WIN SOLUTIONS

AGREE TO HAVE A "BINDING" QUALITY TO THE RESOLUTION

"Fighting fire with fire only gets you ashes."
—*Abigail Van Buren*

THE PROCESS OF CONFLICT RESOLUTION

Resolving conflict can be a trained and practiced approach. Below is a suggested method for conflict resolution. It involves analyzing the source of conflict and openly discussing the issues with assertive, non-aggressive communication before developing ideas and opinions and finally agreeing on mutually acceptable solutions.

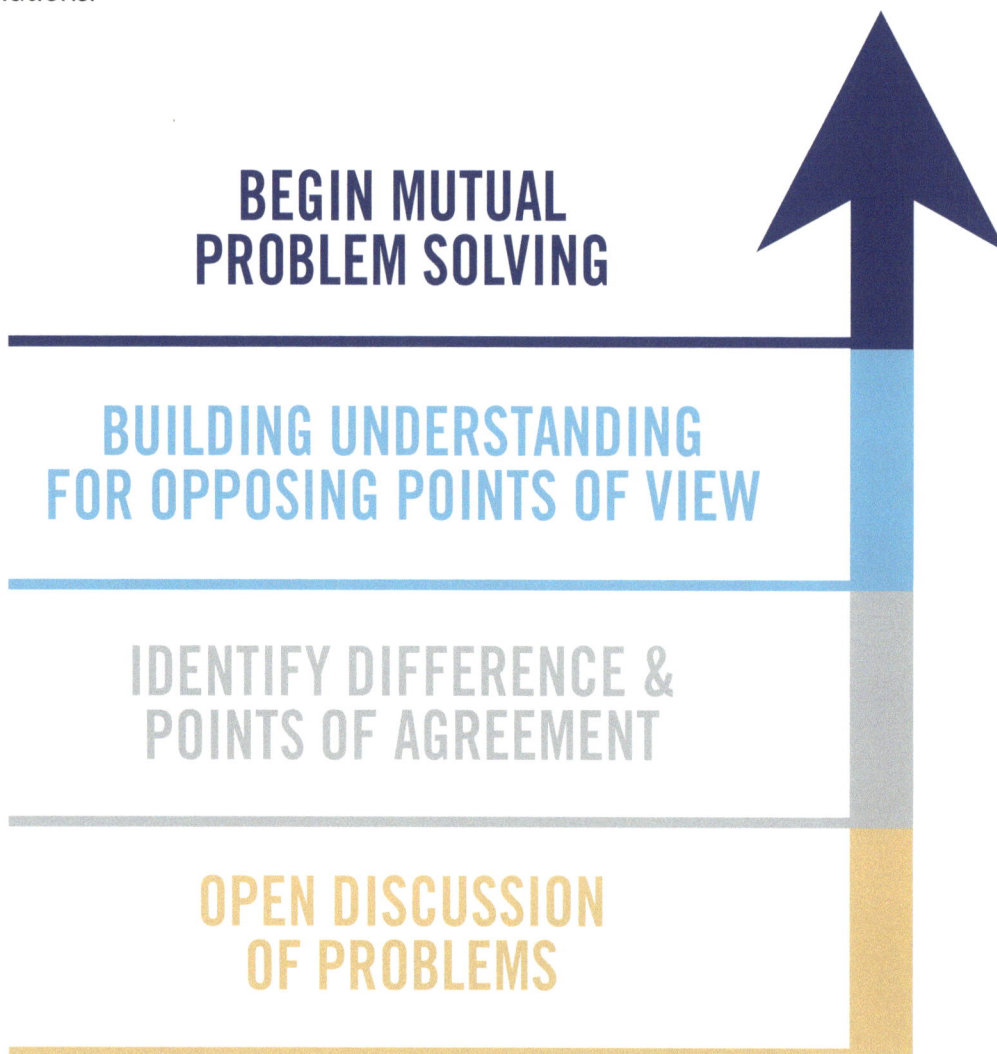

BEGIN MUTUAL PROBLEM SOLVING

BUILDING UNDERSTANDING FOR OPPOSING POINTS OF VIEW

IDENTIFY DIFFERENCE & POINTS OF AGREEMENT

OPEN DISCUSSION OF PROBLEMS

"Conflict isn't bad for organizations: it's fundamental to them. The ability to work through opposing sides of an issue and come to a resolution is in the best interest of customers, shareholders, and employees." — Liane Davey,

The Good Fight: Use Productive Conflict to Get Your Team and Organization Back on Track

THE PROCESS OF CONFLICT RESOLUTION

BEGIN MUTUAL PROBLEM SOLVING

✓ What is the worst possible consequence if this conflict is:
  • Never addressed? Addressed and not resolved?
✓ Develop "Doables"
  • Specific actions, based upon shared information from all
  • Ideas generated that have the best chance for success
  • Steps that do not promote an unfair advantage for any particular person
  • Solutions that build trust

BUILDING UNDERSTANDING FOR OPPOSING POINTS OF VIEW

✓ Clarify individual perceptions involved in the conflict.
✓ Clarify what, if any, values are involved in the conflict?
✓ How do the personalities of the people involved impact your perception of the conflict?

IDENTIFY DIFFERENCE & POINTS OF AGREEMENT

✓ List shared needs. Realize that each party needs the other(s) to successfully resolve a conflict. Each party should be concerned with others' needs as well as their own.

OPEN DISCUSSION OF PROBLEMS

✓ Clarify that conflict exists
✓ What are the issues involved in the conflict?
✓ For whom is this a conflict? Each person should define the conflict
✓ Under what circumstances does the conflict manifest itself? For how long?
✓ Assure that each party recognizes that all parties must be involved in the solution for the process to be most effective
✓ What are the hidden issues, below the surface, in this conflict?

BUILDING A CONFLICT MAP

A Conflict Map can be used to manage the resolution process. Such maps ensure that both parties obtain a full overview of the conflict situation, clarify the issues involved, highlight their needs and concerns, and identify ways to move toward agreement.

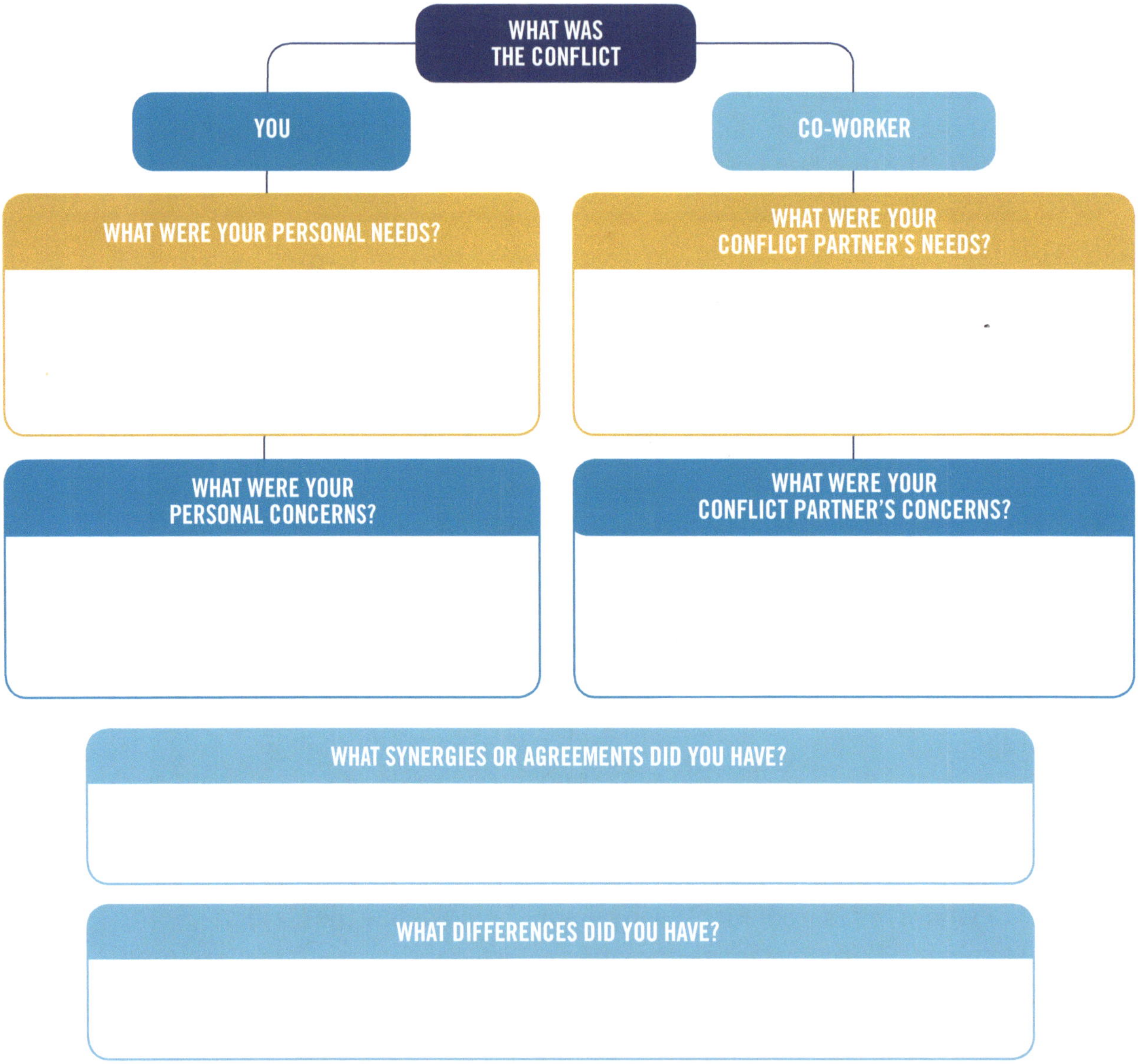

WHAT WAS THE CONFLICT

YOU

CO-WORKER

WHAT WERE YOUR PERSONAL NEEDS?

WHAT WERE YOUR CONFLICT PARTNER'S NEEDS?

WHAT WERE YOUR PERSONAL CONCERNS?

WHAT WERE YOUR CONFLICT PARTNER'S CONCERNS?

WHAT SYNERGIES OR AGREEMENTS DID YOU HAVE?

WHAT DIFFERENCES DID YOU HAVE?

What is a conflict you've had at work that you regretted?

What would you have done differently if you could have a conflict do-over?

What conflict have you been avoiding at work, and why have you been avoiding it?

LISTENING

DISTRACTING ENVIRONMENT

EMOTIONS

SEMANTICS

IMPATIENCE

DISINTEREST

Are you really listening, or simply waiting for your turn to talk?

In addition to applying some of the tips provided on the last page, good listening requires that you are skilled at questioning, and able to accurately reflect back what you heard.

QUESTION

Broadly, there are two types of questions; open-ended and close-ended. Close-ended have a limited range of answers, typically *yes* or *no*. They often begin with *Did you, Will you, Can you, etc.*

Open-ended are effective for gathering much more information. They often begin with words such as *describe, explain, characterize, etc.*

REFLECT

One way to ensure that you've accurately heard the message is to paraphrase what was said. *Paraphrasing* is simply restating what you've heard, but in your own words.

GOOD PARAPHRASING PHRASES INCLUDES:

-))) In other words...

-))) So what you mean is...

-))) I gather that...

-))) If I understand what you are saying...

-))) What I hear you saying is...

-))) Let me see if I understand you correctly...

NOTE: DON'T ask employees if they understood you. The answer will almost always be *YES.* Nobody wants the boss to think they're stupid or weren't listening! DO ask them what questions they have. DO ask them to repeat back what they heard just to be sure you're on the same page.

EMOTIONAL INTELLIGENCE

Emotional Intelligence is a set of skills that allows you to recognize and manage your emotions and the emotional state of other people in order to have appropriate and productive business interactions.

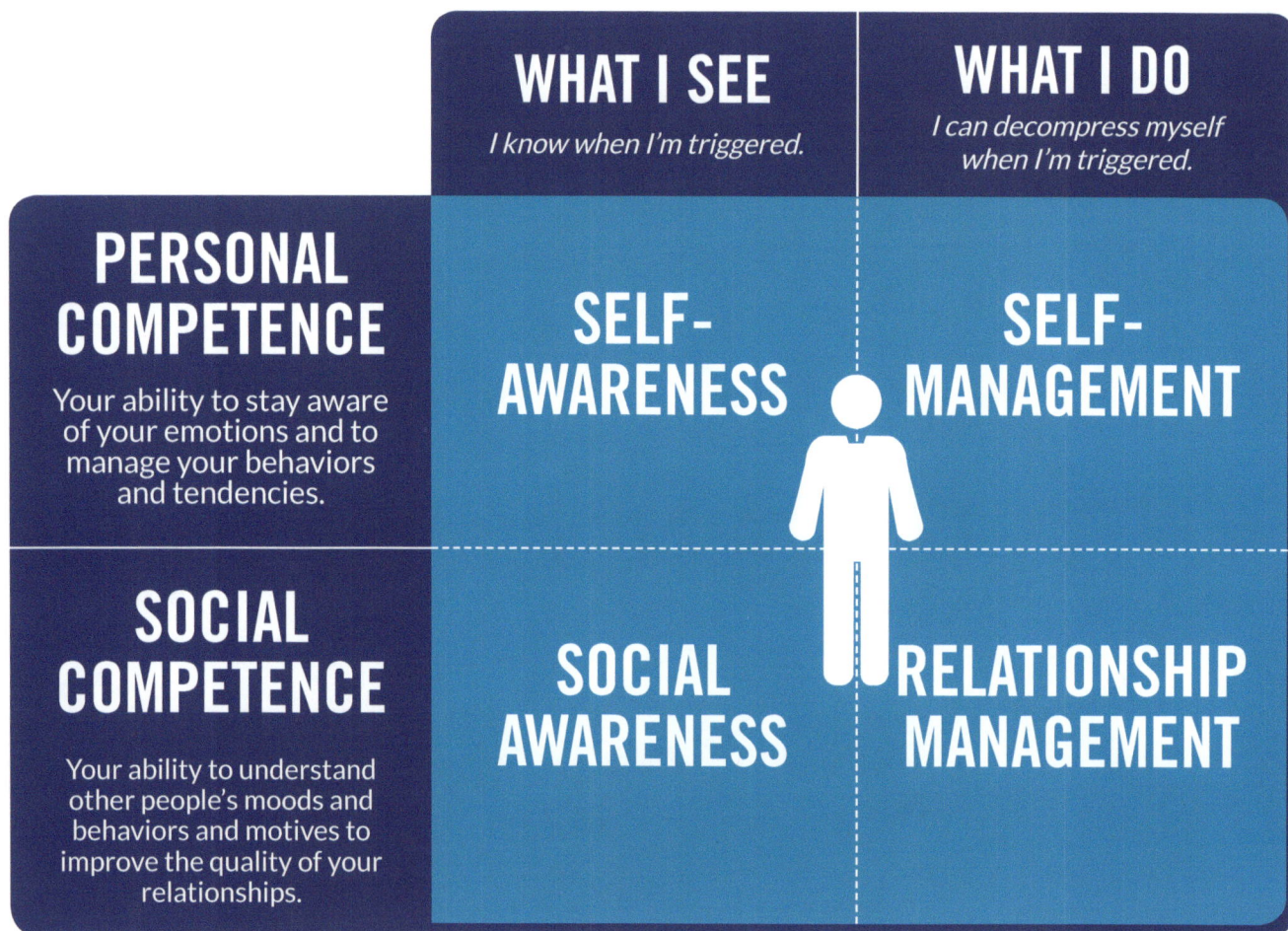

	WHAT I SEE *I know when I'm triggered.*	**WHAT I DO** *I can decompress myself when I'm triggered.*
PERSONAL COMPETENCE Your ability to stay aware of your emotions and to manage your behaviors and tendencies.	**SELF-AWARENESS**	**SELF-MANAGEMENT**
SOCIAL COMPETENCE Your ability to understand other people's moods and behaviors and motives to improve the quality of your relationships.	**SOCIAL AWARENESS**	**RELATIONSHIP MANAGEMENT**

How good are you at managing your own emotions?
How good are you at managing the emotions of others?

① RESPOND WITH EMOTIONAL INTELLIGENCE

SITUATION: Your boss walks into your area and informs you that the deadline for the high profile project you're working on has been accelerated. You know that this means you and your team will have to work even more weekends and nights. Your spouse will not be pleased! As your boss waits for your response, you feel your blood pressure going up to the point that you're literally getting hot around the collar and your mouth is getting dry. It seems like all the work you ever do for this boss is "rush, rush".

UNINTELLIGENT RESPONSE	INTELLIGENT RESPONSE

② RESPOND WITH EMOTIONAL INTELLIGENCE

SITUATION: Three weeks ago Joan transferred to your project team. Her previous boss warned you to expect that she would be frequently late. You've also been told that she tends to get defensive when given constructive feedback. For the first two weeks, everything was fine. But this week she was a half hour late on Monday, Wednesday and again today, Friday. You sense that a few of the other project team members have taken notice, and are wondering how you'll respond. Keep in mind that because of Joan's specialized skills, she is deemed a "critical resource" by the company. You can't afford to lose her, but her lateness seems to be getting out of hand. Frankly, you're feeling disrespected too.

UNINTELLIGENT RESPONSE	INTELLIGENT RESPONSE

LANGUAGE THAT DIFFUSES CONFLICTS

Remember that you are trying to remain neutral. Avoid individual positive reinforcement as much as negative reaction. Praising select individuals can be interpreted as negative feedback to the remaining members.

Use restatement, paraphrasing, and reinforcement for your responses rather than "that's good."

Avoid autobiography. Use examples from your own experiences, but be careful that you don't inappropriately draw attention to yourself and away from a group member.

Use smiles, nods, and comfortable silence. Be encouraging.

- Let me see if I understand….

- Tell me more about that….

- In the interest of time….

- We certainly have come up with a lot of ideas.

- That's interesting.

- So how close are we to agreement?

- So where do we really differ on these points?

- What needs to happen for us to agree?

- How might that work?

- What would it take to resolve this?

- I can see that you have strong feelings about that.

- It sounds like….

- Let me make a suggestion.

- I see.

- Hmmm.

- I think we see the point you're trying to make and I want to make sure our recorder gets it down. Can you "headline" that for me?

- I know we all would like to get to solutions, but can we agree to spend __ minutes on problems first?

- Can I remind you of the agreement we made to… [list of ground rules].

QUESTIONS FOR GOOD CONFLICT MANAGEMENT

QUESTIONS TO OVERCOME YOUR INNER AVERSION TO CONFLICT:

Can we move forward effectively if there are issues that haven't been addressed or resolved?	Is this an important issue to discuss, regardless of how unpleasant the conversation might become?	Would I be better off if I understood how people are thinking and feeling about this issue?

QUESTIONS TO ASSESS WHETHER TO INTERVENE AND NOT TO "MIND YOUR OWN BUSINESS":

Would my intervening help to balance a situation with a power gap?	Could I use my credibility or influence to make the situation better?	Do I have a perspective on the issue that will help open up the potential solutions?

QUESTIONS TO ASSESS IF A CONFLICT WITH YOUR BOSS IS WARRANTED:

I need to do something different from what my boss instructed to be successful?	Will bringing up the issue make it less likely that I'll face negative consequences later?	Would my colleagues thank me for having the courage to raise the issue?

Based on the book,
The Good Fight: Use Productive Conflict to Get Your Team and Organization Back on Track,
by Liane Davey
Visit www.LianeDavey.com to learn more

TECHNIQUES TO DIFFUSE CONFLICTS

Shoe Stepping: Use this approach to put yourself in the shoes of the person with whom you're engaged with a conflict, which may help you value their perspective more. Say, "I'm struggling to understand your perspective and I'd like to, can you tell me more about…"

Going Upstream: This approach will help you understand how the person came to draw the conclusion you might be opposed to. When you know how they formed their opinion or idea, you might become more tolerant of their position. Say, "Help me understand what led you to that conclusion…"

Play it Forward: This technique can be used when you want a person to consider the negative results that can result from their perspective. Getting them to draw their own conclusion is far less threatening than if you bluntly state your opinions about their idea or perspective. "I can see how [restate their idea]. How might that impact [insert your concern]?"

Go With It: What can you do when you just want the person to entertain your idea, even though they are locked into theirs? Say, "I get it, and your probably right [restate their idea]. Just for a moment, though, play with me here. What if I could somehow [resolve their concern], what would be the value of [insert your idea]."

Two Truths: Sometimes the person you're engaged with a conflict is only recognizing their side of the issue. Start by acknowledging the truth of what they said, and then add the truth you hold which is different. Very often two counter-balancing can both be true at the same time. Say, "It's true that…It's also true that…"

Boomerang: One of the best ways to avoid getting into a conflict, is to have other people come to your side before the conflict gets started. Say, "So that I'm clear, your saying [restate their position]. Got it. I wonder if someone else here has a different viewpoint they can share."

What Else: Sometimes the person with which you're engaged in a conflict has a half-baked perspective that, with a little help, could be better. Say, "My understanding of your idea is [restate your understanding of their idea]. So what else do we need to include with this idea? What might be missing?"

THINK WIN/WIN

> "Conflict is a natural part of healthy relationships and a critical defense against unhealthy ones." — *Liane Davey,*
>
> *The Good Fight: Use Productive Conflict to Get Your Team and Organization Back on Track*

TREATING MEETING CONFLICTS PRODUCTIVELY

ACKNOWLEDGING

UNPRODUCTIVE BEHAVIOR

Acknowledging unproductive behavior brings the problem out in the open where you can deal with it. If you ignore the behavior, you indirectly endorse it and the behavior will probably continue.

This technique is simple. In a neutral way, state the facts as you see them. Then ask the group how to correct the unproductive behavior. For example, say,

- "We seem to have drifted off the subject. How does this relate to the issue we're discussing?"
- "We seem to have more than one conversation now. Should we break into smaller discussion groups or can we continue to work on this as a whole?"
- "We've been working on this topic for a while. Everyone looks a little tired. Should we take a break?"
- "We seem to disagree on this issue. Do we need to resolve our differences?"
- "I feel like we're stuck, or at least I am. Can we review the meeting purpose to see if we're still working towards our desired outcome."

Encourage participants to also help acknowledge unproductive behavior. You can set this as a ground rule.

Wording Interventions

The facilitator needs to identify critical moments in the meeting and intervene when appropriate. Your word choice and tone of voice are very important.

PREVENTING CONFLICT IN MEETINGS

Only use 6-8 ground rules for any given meeting.

Choose standard ground rules for recurring meetings. (See section on Improving Team Meetings.)

Review ground rules at beginning of meeting and post for all to see.

Ground rules are your best tool for heading off potential conflict.

GROUND RULES

Ground rules are norms of behavior that the group has agreed to follow. You can call them ground rules, meeting guidelines, team norms, meeting protocols, or expectations. Whatever you call them, USE them. Consistently using ground rules can prevent most of your meeting problems.

First, identify the problems your groups typically have, then have group members agree in advance to follow the ground rules that will head off those problems. Use the following checklist as a start.

- Start, stay, and stop on time (The "S3 Rule")
- Every idea and comment is valid
- Defer judgment on ideas
- Share ideas and experiences
- Take responsibility for the outcome of the meeting
- Seek first to understand, then to be understood
- What's said here, stays here!
- No phone calls or interruptions during the meeting
  (The "100-Mile Rule," that is, pretend you are 100 miles away from the office without phones or computers. Leave the meeting only for those matters you would drive 100 miles to attend to)
- Be patient with the process
- Everyone participates
- Everyone is considered equal.
  (Check your status/level at the door)
- We will strive to reach consensus
- People do not need to agree, only to understand
- Maintain focus – avoid side conversations

WIN AS MUCH AS YOU CAN

INSTRUCTIONS:

For eight consecutive rounds, I group will chose either A or B, and II group will choose either X or Y. The score each group receives in a given round is determined by the pattern made by the choices of both groups. The payoff schedule is listed below:

AX = *Both teams win 3 points*

AY = *Group I loses 6 points, Group II wins 6 points*

BX = *Group I wins 6 points, Group II loses 6 points*

BY = *Both teams lose 3 points*

Round	Minutes	Choice		Cumulative Points	
		Group 1	Group 2	Group 1	Group 2
1	2				
2	2				
3	2 Optional Meeting After Round				
4*	2				
5	2 Optional Meeting After Round				
6**					

In addition to the facilitative language listed earlier,
here are some facilitative phrases to use in difficult situations:

When two people are arguing opposing views and not listening to each other:

"I'm not sure that either of you are hearing the points that the other is making. I'd like to ask you both to hold your own comments and to first restate what the other has said. Let's see how well we're listening to each other." Ask both people to paraphrase the other's point until they are both satisfied that the other person fully understands the point. If this is a recurring problem in your meetings, add "Seek First to Understand, Then to Be Understood" to your list of ground rules.

When one person dominates the discussion:

"Dana, you always have lots of valuable ideas, but we need to hear from the other members of the team. Could you hold that thought until after we've heard from some of the others?"

When a person makes only negative remarks about the ideas of another person:

"Lynne, you've mentioned several reasons why Mark's proposal won't work. What are three things you like about what Mark said?" You may need to coax Lynne to pull out the positive comments.

When team members are not following the ground rules they previously agreed to:

"Let's pause for a moment and look back at the ground rules we agreed to earlier. Are we following them? Should we make any changes to our list or add any new ones?"

"Far and away the best prize that life has to offer is the chance to work hard at work worth doing."
—*Theodore Roosevelt*

TREATING MEETING CONFLICTS PRODUCTIVELY

WHEN ONE PERSON IS PERSONALLY ATTACKING ANOTHER:

Personal attacks hurt people and can kill the meeting. Use the escalating scale of intervention below to control and stop the attacker. Start at the bottom with low-level interventions and use higher-level interventions only as necessary.

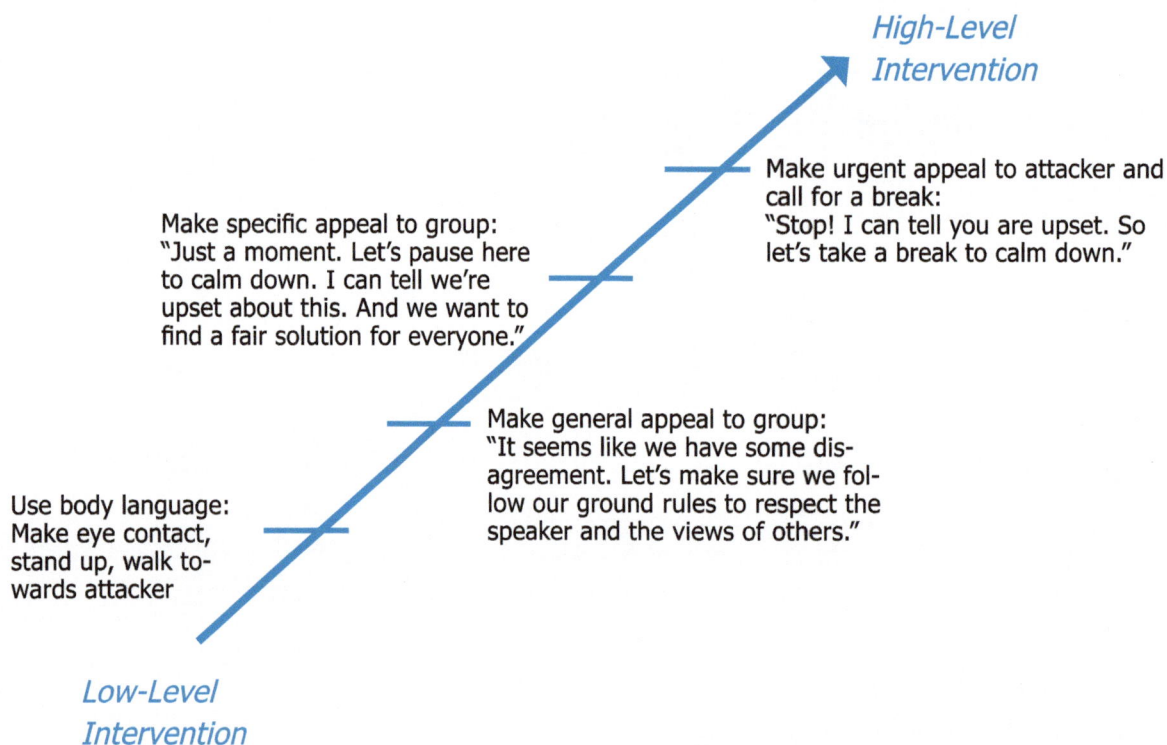

High-Level Intervention

Make urgent appeal to attacker and call for a break:
"Stop! I can tell you are upset. So let's take a break to calm down."

Make specific appeal to group:
"Just a moment. Let's pause here to calm down. I can tell we're upset about this. And we want to find a fair solution for everyone."

Make general appeal to group:
"It seems like we have some disagreement. Let's make sure we follow our ground rules to respect the speaker and the views of others."

Use body language:
Make eye contact, stand up, walk towards attacker

Low-Level Intervention

If you have to call a break to stop the attack, remain objective when you coach the attacker. Focus on specific behavior, not personalities. For example, do not say, "Greg, you were mean to Diana." Instead, state what you observed and link the behavior to the negative results. For example, say, "Greg, when you criticized Diana's ideas, I think you got a little personal and hurt her feelings. We all want to get to the right solution here. What do you think we should do to smooth things over and get back on track?"

11 RULES FOR LOW CONFLICT MEETINGS

1 Put people first

2 Include everyone

3 Present a compelling vision

4 Outline clear performance goals

5 Keep everyone focused on one plan

6 Facts and data drive decisions

7 Propose a plan, "find-a-way" attitude

8 Respect, listen, help, and appreciate each other

9 Emotional resilience ... trust the process

10 Have fun ... enjoy the journey and each other

11 ...no side discussions, no jokes at anyone else's expense, no Smart phones, & no computers

- Alan Mulally, former CEO Ford Motor Company

NOTES

Dear clients and friends,

You are the focus of everything we do at Giant Leap Consulting. When you leave a Giant Leap workshop, seminar or keynote, you will be armed with practical strategies and tools that you can immediately put to use back at work. As I often tell our clients, the person leaving our training programs should not be the same person who entered it. You deserve to be more confident, skilled and capable after experiencing a Giant Leap program.

Since our founding in 2002, Giant Leap has been fortunate to have worked with thousands of executives from some of the best organizations in the world. You've taught us a lot about what works – and what doesn't – when it comes to adult learners. You can count on us to always provide learning experiences that have rich content, insightful dialogue, engaging activities, and relevant case studies.

There's something else you can count on too: first-rate course materials. Our participant notebooks, PowerPoints, and course materials are among the best in the world. I know that's a tall claim, but it's true! You can sample our course material and see for yourself! – just send an email to info@giantleapconsulting.com.

Please take a moment to immerse yourself in Giant Leap's new course catalogue. In addition to introducing our tried-and-true training courses, it also showcases our two "signature" programs: Courageous Leadership, and Open-door Leadership.

Stay Courageous!

Bill Treasurer

Bill Treasurer, Chief Encouragement Officer,
Giant Leap Consulting, Inc.

P.S. Need a customized course? Giant Leap loves to develop new and original content for our clients!

Contact: info@giantleapconsulting.com

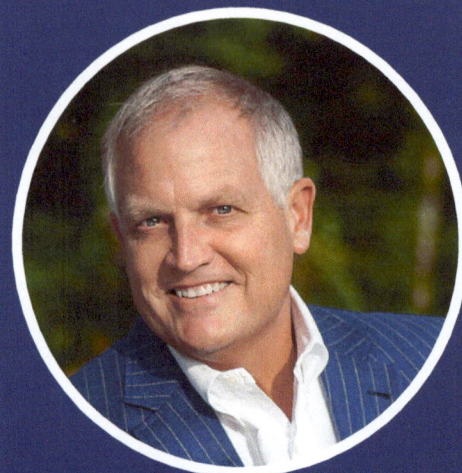

ABOUT BILL'S KEYNOTES

In the past two decades, thousands of executives across the globe have attended Bill's keynotes and workshops. Benefiting from the concepts first introduced in Bill's bestselling books, participants come away with stronger leadership skills, improved team performance, and more career backbone.

Among others, Bill has led workshops for NASA, Accenture, Lenovo, USB Bank, CNN, Hugo Boss, SPANX, the Centers for Disease Control and Prevention, the U.S. Department of Veterans Affairs, and the Pittsburgh Pirates.

Bill's insights about courage and risk-taking have been featured in over 100 newspapers and magazines, including the Washington Post, NY Daily News, Chicago Tribune, Atlanta Journal Constitution, Boston Herald, Woman's Day, Redbook, Fitness, and The Harvard Management Update.

Little Leaps Press, Inc.
2 Lynwood Road
Asheville, NC 28804

Bulk Order Sales: Special discounts may be available for large quantity sales. For details, call: 800-867-7239.

Title: Unlocking Horns: Courageous Conflict at Work
Author: Bill Treasurer
Publication Date: June 1, 2019
Publisher: Little Leaps Press, Inc.

Published in the United States of America
by Little Leaps Press, Inc.
ISBN: 978-1-948058-21-6

LITTLE LEAPS
PRESS

www.ingramcontent.com/pod-product-compliance
Lightning Source LLC
Chambersburg PA
CBHW041703200326
41518CB00002B/179

9 781948 058216